C000094020

Thankfully, this book will be your little helper over the duration of planning the stag do. From knowing where to start and choosing the guest list to offering activity ideas and ways to make the event cheaper, this stag do planning guide will help you leap over the obstacles that you experience along the way and host a stag do that will be remembered by the groom and your fellow stags for years to come.

# MAKING A PLAN

ALWAYS PLAN AHEAD.
IT WASN'T RAINING WHEN
NOAH BUILT THE ARK.

★ *Richard Cushing* ★

# STAG
# DO

## *planning*
# GUIDE

### Dan Bridges

summersdale

STAG DO PLANNING GUIDE

Summersdale Publishers Ltd
46 West Street
Chichester
West Sussex
PO19 1RP
UK

www.summersdale.com

Printed and bound in Malta

ISBN: 978-1-78685-010-2

Substantial discounts on bulk quantities of Summersdale books are available to corporations, professional associations and other organisations. For details contact general enquiries: telephone: +44 (0) 1243 771107, fax: +44 (0) 1243 786300 or email: enquiries@summersdale.com.

Disclaimer: The publisher cannot be held responsible for any loss or claim arising out of the use, or misuse, of the suggestions made herein. Please take all necessary precautions and seek the advice of qualified professionals when engaging in potentially dangerous activities.

# CONTENTS

# INTRODUCTION

So, you've been tasked with organising a stag do. Are you the sole organiser? Do you have helpers? Are you in charge of five or 35 guests? Does the groom-to-be want to go abroad? For a week? A weekend? Does he want to keep it local and just go to a nearby pub and for a bite to eat at a restaurant? Or maybe he wants to head into the wilderness where he can truly relax and be at one with nature? Perhaps you are the groom-to-be and you'd rather organise things yourself? There are many conversations to be had and decisions to be made!

The number of guests and desired activities will greatly affect the amount of effort required of you, the organiser. Sorting a stag do might look like hard work, but it should ultimately be enjoyable – if you start to feel stressed you may find you need an extra pair of hands to help out. Don't be afraid to ask the groom-to-be to designate another helper if you're feeling overwhelmed.

Most men would usually cower at the thought of planning an event that involved a group of other men – some strangers, some not – and which was, for the groom-to-be, the most highly anticipated day of their year (of course, with the exception of his wedding!). So, when you're asked to be the best man of a close friend or relative it can feel like a lot of responsibility is sitting heavily on your shoulders. But if you start planning early and make sure each stage is accounted for, there will be no need to panic. The key is to wangle as much information out of your stag as you possibly can in terms of their interests and the interests of the others they want to invite. If half of the guests have families and responsibilities back home, they might not be able to attend a do abroad. Be as open-minded as possible and don't let your vision overshadow that of the groom-to-be's. It is his time to relax, after all.

# SIT DOWN WITH THE GROOM-TO-BE

Don't become the male stereotype and leave everything to the last minute when it comes to organising the do; make sure you give yourself and the groom-to-be enough time to run through the basics before you take full control of the planning.

Sit down with a beer – this often helps the flow of ideas – and come up with a few potential dates. Most stag dos are organised to take place a few weeks before the big day, so that when it comes to the groom having to say his vows, the events of the party seem like a very distant memory. More traditionally, you could celebrate your stag's last hours of singledom the night before the wedding, as a lot of grooms-to-be were accustomed to, but do you really want to take that risk?!

Unfortunately, you can't please everyone and some people whom you invite won't be able to make it, but once you've settled on the dates with the stag it's best to stick to them as changing them to be flexible with the guests can create confusion and more planning (which you really don't want!). The more notice you give your guests, the more likely most of them will be able to make it. And when it comes to booking accommodation, activities and travel, you want to get in there before everything is booked up.

Ask for a rough idea of what he'd like to do – bearing in mind the demographics of the guests too. Does he want to go abroad or stay closer to home? What sort of day/ weekend does he have in mind? More sophisticated, packed full of activities and potentially a little pricey, or cheap and cheerful and to a strict budget?

# HOW TO SORT THE GUEST LIST

The groom-to-be will want to celebrate his do with his nearest and dearest, and those who know how to have a belter. Speak to him about who you should invite, bearing in mind that smaller group activities are easier to organise and often more intimate. Although his requests should be considered, sometimes you will need to gently intervene so that you can make the event possible – if he wants to invite all 100 of his Facebook friends of varying ages, interests and bank balances you will have to let him down lightly.

It is becoming more popular for the stag's father to attend, and even the bride-to-be's! This requires a lot of thought before a decision should be made. For example, what is the general demographic of your guests? And will they want to go clubbing after having partaken in white-water rafting and a skydive in the same day? Perhaps a separate more formal occasion should be arranged by the groom-to-be as an alternative.

When you've put together a potential guest list quickly check through it to make sure there won't be any unexpected meetings for your guests. If you think that there are certain guests who don't see eye-to-eye and it could cause tension, speak to the groom-to-be to see how best to approach the situation.

Once you've got a clear idea of what kind of event it's going to be, gather the contact details of all those invited (the groom-to-be should be able to supply you with these) and send out a 'save the date' invitation. Introduce yourself, let them know they have been invited to a stag do and add a sentence or two about what that might entail. Ask them to RSVP by a certain date – a week or two in the future should give them enough time – and chase them if they haven't replied by this date.

# HOW TO CONTACT GUESTS

★ Email

★ Letter with perforated RSVP

★ Postcard with picture of the stag

★ Social media group

★ WhatsApp group

★ Group text message

## STAG HACK

Rather than finding your inbox flooded with RSVPs from stags, ask them to fill in a quick and simple online poll to determine who is available when. Doodle.com is a good tool for this: simply follow the instructions, add the potential party dates and email the link to the stags. Once everyone has filled it in, you'll be able to see which dates are the most popular and when would be best to hold the party.

## SAMPLE EMAIL TO STAGS

Dear Stags,

Some of you know me, but for those who don't – Hi! I'm [insert groom-to-be's name here]'s best friend/brother/best man and have been asked to sort out his stag do, to which you have been invited!

We're looking at a few dates in [insert month(s) here] and it would be great if you could follow this link and let me know your availability [insert Doodle poll link here].

[Insert groom-to-be's name here] is keen to spend a weekend in [European destination]/[name of home city] [delete/add as applicable] and would love for you to join in on the fun ahead of his big day.

I hope you can make it and look forward to hearing from you.

[insert your name here]

## BUDGET

Decide on a budget with the groom-to-be; be sensible – if the stags earn wildly varying amounts, be sympathetic to that and keep it cheap. The ones who earn loads can buy in the bubbly if they want to make an extra contribution.

# MAKE RULES AND STICK TO THEM

★ Decide whether or not a ban should be placed on uploading photos ('risky' or not) to the internet.

★ Perhaps the stags should 'buddy up' to stop each other from drunk-dialling or uploading aforementioned banned photos to the internet.

★ In the unlikely event that anyone falls out with the groom-to-be or you notice tension building – for example a disgruntled guest who's had one beer too many – be ready to defuse the situation. This is the groom-to-be's special weekend and a ruckus won't ever be forgotten.

## HOW MUCH TO TELL THE STAG

Make sure you are clear on how much the groom-to-be wants to know about the weekend and what he would prefer to be kept as a surprise. He may want to be involved every step of the way, in which case you might want to organise some smaller surprises – maybe a special outfit for him to wear or a gift from all his stags. Above all, make sure any surprises will go down well – that may mean sounding out any ideas with his loved ones or the other stags just to make sure.

# CHECKLIST

Before you do anything else, make a list of what needs to be done and in what order. Your list should look something like this:

★ Decide possible dates with groom-to-be

★ Gather list of stags' contact details from groom-to-be

★ Send out an email to stags to check they are available

★ Sit down with the groom-to-be to discuss particulars

★ Do your research

★ Communicate with the guests about budget/loose plans so far

★ Do some more research with the above in mind

★ Set a detailed budget

★ Book accommodation and gather funds from stags

★ Book activities and gather funds from stags

★ Assign jobs to other stags if needs be

★ Send out an itinerary and accommodation details, including requests for any props etc. the stags need to bring with them

★ Send an email to all the stags the week before the event, just to check everyone is prepared and has all the information they need.

# THEMES

# THEME:
# BOOZY

---

**BEER SEEMS LIKE AN EVEN BETTER IDEA AFTER YOU'VE HAD SOME BEER.**

★ *Steven Hall* ★

---

Is the stag up to his eyeballs in wedding talk and making sure everything is perfect for the big day? Perhaps he needs a big boozy break from it all, where the word 'drink' is a perpetual siren that by the end of the do will be feared by all. From a brewery tour in the morning to shots before you stumble home at 4 a.m., you can make sure you'll always have a pint in your hand with these activities.

# DAYTIME ACTIVITIES

## BREWERY EXPERIENCE

Take a tour around a brewery and learn about the process of beer-making. A typical experience includes a greeting from the owner and an expert guide, who will accompany you around the brewery explaining everything, from ingredients to equipment, and then, finally, tasting the different types of beer. If the stag is a bit of a foodie too, look out for experiences that couple food and beer-tasting where, in addition, you'll learn which foods complement which beers. What's more, if the groom-to-be isn't all that keen on beer there are other types of boozy experiences, such as distillery and cider mill tours.

# BEER BIKE

If you are going to a city you've never been to before but you're left with the predicament of whether you should sightsee or head straight to the bar, there's no need to fret as you can accomplish both via a beer bike. This activity has seen a rise in popularity, especially in typical European stag-do destinations, and is a great warming-up session before the evening antics begin. Plus, you'll be able to capture some good photographs to prove that you did something other than sit in a pub all weekend. The bike comes with a guide and someone to steer – so you don't have to worry about navigating – a barrel of beer and pedals so you can sit back with a drink, do some light exercise and be a typical tourist (well, sort of). The bikes tend to cater for smaller groups of five to eight 'riders', however, some companies do offer bigger bikes for bigger groups, but this would need to be discussed with them at the earliest possible time.

## BEER-GOGGLE FOOTBALL

Although this activity doesn't require necking drinks, it'll certainly feel like you have as you try to play football, practise techniques and win challenges with warped vision that'll send you spinning. There will be many fails and falls, and after the session ends you'll be requesting a pint at the bar to see straight again.

## CRUISING FOR A BOOZING

If you are lucky and aren't limited to a certain budget, you might want to book a boozy boat cruise. You will get the option of going in the day or at night, but if you want to make the most of taking in the scenery then go for the former. There are countless experiences to choose from, whether it's an intimate affair on a small boat or a club that just happens to be floating on water, so make sure it's something that the stag and guests will most appreciate. And when you go to book, make sure you know exactly what is included and what is not, and how much drinks are if they aren't included in the cost of the cruise – you wouldn't want your guests to get the hump with you for having to spend a fortune on a pint.

# EVENING ACTIVITIES

## BAR CRAWL

Probably the most obvious activity for a stag do and something you can organise yourself, although there are some companies that can do it for you. (Check with your guests before you sign up to this, as they may not be too enthused about spending money on something that can be easily organised independently.) Make sure you research the pubs and bars and their locations and work out a route ahead of time. Also, remember that you will be drinking a lot over a long time – unless you crash, of course – so it's worth booking a table at a restaurant before the crawl begins, giving them plenty of notice, to help line your stomachs and prolong the drinking time.

# PARTY BUS

Step on board your exclusive party bus and cruise along city streets with drinks on tap and music pumping. Stop at different bars along the way and enjoy beating the queues with your VIP passes. If you want to hire a sexy stripper for your stag, this might be a good opportunity to do so as bus companies usually offer this experience as an extra.

# STAG HACK

Get everyone in the party mood with personalised T-shirts. You'll need enough cheap plain black T-shirts for your guests, some transfer paper, parchment paper and an inkjet printer. If you don't have a printer, at least one of the stags should have one. Alternatively, go to your local library and use the printers there.

Once you know how much the materials cost, let the guests know so they can chip in. Find the most awful photo of the stag you can (usually Facebook goes above and beyond this remit) and save it as an image. Open the photo with your preferred viewer and select the size you want it to be on the T-shirts. Then print the design on to the transfer paper and leave to dry for 30 minutes. Cut out the photo and peel the double-sided paper apart, discarding the blank piece. Place the design on the T-shirt and on top of that lay a piece of parchment paper. Then iron away, reaching the edges of the design so that it sticks properly.

Note: Although these are sound instructions, always refer to the guide that comes with the transfer paper as different brands offer varying advice.

# COMEDY NIGHT

Whether you opt for a household name or an upcoming star, a comedy night can tick a lot of boxes for a group of stags. Everyone likes to have a laugh and there's no better way to do this than at a stand-up show. Also, if some of your guests don't like to drink, this is the perfect place for them to sip on their $H_2O$ and still have a good time. A smaller venue may benefit you more than going to a sell-out arena as they tend to be more comfortable. For example, they usually provide tables for your party to sit around, as opposed to sitting in an orderly straight line, and it's easier to grab a drink from the bar – you don't have to wait for the interval and load up with as many plastic cups as you can possibly carry. If the stags don't all know each other well yet, this is also a perfect opportunity to break the ice, before the night begins and you all start to embarrass yourselves.

# ESSENTIAL KIT

★ Your game face

★ A good sense of humour

★ Some crazy dares and fun drinking games

★ Paracetamol for sore heads the following morning

# FANCY DRESS IDEAS

★ Personalised T-shirts

★ Nun outfits

★ Morphsuits (although think this one through carefully)

★ An inflatable willy costume for the stag (sperm outfits for the guests, optional)

# THEME: ADRENALINE JUNKIE

---

**ANYTHING THAT GETS YOUR BLOOD RACING IS PROBABLY WORTH DOING.**

★ *Hunter S. Thompson* ★

---

A stag do is about celebrating the groom-to-be's life; so why not take this to the next level and live for today as you hit euphoric highs, and get your blood pumping and your adrenaline rushing. Although the activities in this section will be pricier than your average pint down the pub, they are guaranteed to give the stag a weekend he'll never forget.

# DAYTIME ACTIVITIES

## SKYDIVE

There's nothing more breathtaking than freefalling through the air, watching the world as you make your descent, and then feeling that burst of adrenaline as the parachute opens and you can enjoy the spectacular views. To surprise (or scare the shit out of) the groom-to-be, make sure he's blindfolded until he reaches the venue and then record his face as he realises where he is and what he has to do. For most parties, the skydive will be too expensive for everyone to do, but to make the stag's day, or weekend, you could all chip in for the cost of his jump. No doubt it'll be worth the money just seeing his video played back once he's back on the ground.

Alternatively, there is also the option of booking an indoor skydive, which is a fraction of the price and won't get your stomach churning as much.

# BUNGEE JUMP

Fancy seeing the groom-to-be strapped up to a rope of elastic bands and flinging himself off a ledge into the abyss? Bungee jumping is the daddy of adrenaline sports as the catch is you have to do the jump all by yourself. The heights of jumps vary and everyone is guaranteed to be entertained by the high-pitched cries the stag makes as he takes the plunge.

# COASTEERING

This is an activity that is more group-friendly, as you become a team and tackle the jagged coastlines, scrambling up and down rocks, cliff-jumping and then swimming to safety. Although you will be led by an experienced instructor, make sure that all the guests are fit and healthy and have no underlying illnesses. This is a great way to bring the group together and will give you lots to talk about for the rest of the day.

Canyoning is a similar activity which combines abseiling, jumping off waterfalls, swimming and climbing in beautiful natural areas. Both canyoning and coasteering are great fun and are around the same price.

## THEME PARK

Test the limits of your wild side (and your stomach) by spending the day at a theme park and see how many loop the loops, drops and corkscrews you can handle. If you're going to a local theme park, check out the deals on offer – there are usually plenty – and make sure you choose a date that doesn't fall on its closed period during the winter months. It's also worth avoiding school holidays and weekends if possible, as these are peak times and can be very busy.

## ZORBING

If you haven't done it before, now is definitely your chance to tick it off the bucket list. You have the option of rolling down a huge hill in an inflatable ball without brakes on your own or, even better, in a pair. If you want to take it up a notch, some companies offer hydro zorbing with added water, but for most the fun is seeing your fellow zorbing partner's face as you scream and laugh your way down the hill.

# EVENING ACTIVITIES

## GHOST TOUR/ZOMBIE EXPERIENCE

If your adrenaline levels are dipping from the morning's skydive, grab yourself a quick boost with a spooktacular guided walk or organise a terror attraction that'll scare the group out of their wits. Generally, there are more activities to choose from in the run-up to Halloween but many cities offer something terrifying all year round. This is also a great opportunity to dress for the occasion and not only be scared by the experience but also make it your mission to scare each other. Zombie costumes are ideal and require little effort. Wear old clothes that you don't mind ruining and apply fake blood onto them. For an authentic look, buy some face paints and take it in turns to make each other look like the undead.

## JAMES-BOND-THEMED NIGHT

Get suited and booted and remember to take a form of ID as your licence to thrill as you hit the town in style. Hire a flash car, take a detour to a casino to splash the cash (or head to the penny slot machines), then off to a swanky bar for some Martinis – shaken not stirred, of course. And don't forget to book your VIP spaces for the nightclub – that's if you make it there after all those potent cocktails.

# STAG HACK

## Make a James Bond-worthy Martini

Save some money by setting up a makeshift cocktail bar at home, or in a nominated house, and get each of the guests whipping up a fine beverage with this Martini recipe:

Required: 120 ml gin, 35 ml vermouth, 1 olive, cocktail shaker, strainer, ice

1. Add ice to the shaker.

2. Pour in the dry vermouth, shake to infuse the flavours and strain.

3. Add the gin of your choice; a good-quality brand and strength will impact the overall quality of the drink.

4. Stir or shake à la James Bond – ironically, experts favour stirring, as this method doesn't cloud the drink – until the shaker is cold and strain into the glass.

5. Garnish with an olive and sip with the effortless bravado of a true spy.

## ESSENTIAL KIT

★ No fear

★ A heart made of steel

★ A GoPro to capture the events of the day

★ Comfortable clothing

## FANCY DRESS IDEAS

★ 007

★ Superheroes

★ Ghosts and zombies

# THEME: GREAT OUTDOORS

---

## I AM UNBOREABLE IN THE GREAT OUTDOORS.

★ *P. J. O'Rourke* ★

---

If you know that the groom-to-be likes nothing more than to be out in the fresh air, then pay attention to this section. From going back to basics with bushcraft or taking aim with some clay pigeon shooting, you could really go to town (by going to the countryside) if you think this would be up your stag's street (or, muddy lane).

# DAYTIME ACTIVITIES

## BUSHCRAFT

Building fires, constructing shelters, making traps for your evening's dinner, or catching it yourself – if there ever was an archetypal guys' weekend away, then this is it. If you know the stag doesn't want the chaos and drama of a city do, transport him to the wilderness where there are no interruptions and you can spend some quality time as a group. There are plenty of companies to choose from due to the increasing popularity of bushcraft breaks, and options range from a couple of hours to half and full days.

# WHITE WATER RAFTING

If the groom-to-be is a bit of an adrenaline junkie and loves the outdoors, white water rafting could be the perfect activity. You are guaranteed lots of laughs from getting wet as you paddle against rapids and try not to fall out when you reach a waterfall. The inflatable boats usually hold six to seven people and around the course you'll have an experienced instructor teaching you the strokes and techniques of manoeuvring your vessel.

# CLAY PIGEON SHOOTING

Does an afternoon of shooting sound like something the groom-to-be would enjoy? This is the ultimate hand–eye coordination test and everyone knows there is only one spot for first place, which is when the competition heats up. You could add a little extra jeopardy to the shooting competition by allowing the winner to make up a dare for the loser to complete. If you think the group might have a competitive streak, you could couple this activity with archery. By the end of the day, you might need to organise a massage for those aching arms. That sounds like a good forfeit to me!

# EVENING ACTIVITIES

## NIGHT-TIME WALK

As well as having the whole countryside to yourselves – the chances of others being there are pretty slim – there are many benefits to taking a stroll in the countryside at night-time. Firstly, without daylight, your senses are heightened and you'll have a greater feeling of being at one with nature. Secondly, a walk by torchlight gives you the opportunity to see wildlife you have never stumbled upon before, such as badgers and bats. So find a good spot, take a map, a compass and a torch, and work as a team to find your way around – let the sense of adventure take over!

## STARGAZING

Be at one with nature and settle down on the cool grass to watch the night sky put on a dazzling performance. In the isolated, quiet surroundings you'll be able to really relax – something the stag might appreciate more than you think – and let go of all the pent-up stress. If you aren't astronomy aficionados you may benefit from booking with a company, which will set you up with an expert guide, or the National Trust offers events throughout the year.

# STAG HACK

## Tips for first-time stargazers

★ Check the phase of the moon – stargazing is best done just before a full moon.

★ Take a mat to lie on and some warm clothing. A flask with tea, coffee or a hot toddy will also help to warm you up on a cold night.

★ Apps such as Star Walk (iPhone) or Google Sky (android) will tell you what stars you can see from your current location and a compass will help you navigate the skies.

★ If you have a good quality camera you may be able to take some incredible photos. A tripod will help too.

★ If you have travelled a long way, don't forget to book some nearby accommodation so that you don't have to drive back late at night.

# CAMPING

Some people loathe camping, but no one can deny that luxury camping, or glamping, is a comfortable and affordable way to pass a fun weekend. Gauge what the majority of the group wants to do, roughing it or sleeping in style, giving them a good idea of costs so everyone can make an informed decision based on their budgets.

The activities you can do while camping are endless, as you have so much freedom, but always make sure you are considerate of others within the vicinity. Starting a campfire is a must but make sure they are allowed where you are staying before you begin to build one. A barbecue is a great way to feed a big group and campsites usually have these facilities, although always double check before you turn up with heaps of sausages and burgers. It's best to organise food arrangements and buy everything you need before you arrive at your location as shops are usually limited near campsites. For dessert, go back to your days of yore and toast marshmallows on the campfire, or go one step further and create s'mores by sandwiching toasted marshmallows between two chocolate digestives. End the night, having a drink, playing some games and reminiscing on the groom-to-be's heady, single years.

## ESSENTIAL KIT

★ Warm, comfortable clothing and suitable footwear

★ A torch, a compass

★ A sense of adventure

## FANCY DRESS

★ Medieval

★ Robin Hood

★ Camouflage

# THEME: CULTURED

---

**THIS WORLD IS BUT A CANVAS TO OUR IMAGINATION.**

★ *Henry David Thoreau* ★

---

If your groom-to-be likes the finer things in life, then indulge his tastes with a cultured weekend away. From the razzle dazzle of musicals and the theatre to the modest price tags of galleries and museums (which often don't have price tags at all), you will always be able to find an activity for the groom-to-be and your fellow stags home or away that fits the budget and guarantees a good time.

## DAYTIME ACTIVITIES

## LIFE DRAWING

There may be some stifled laughs and titters from the group as you first lay eyes on the nude model, but halfway into the session you'll all be thinking you are Picassos in the making. Life drawing is a great therapeutic activity, but must be approached with an open mind. To make things competitive, at the end of the session you could ask the model which drawing they think is the most representative. The winner receives a prize.

## SCAVENGER HUNT

A plethora of companies offer both ready-made and tailor-made scavenger hunts for large groups, relevant to your chosen location. A cheaper alternative is to come up with the hunt yourself, or alternatively write a quiz that relates to the stag weekend destination, which would involve the group having to explore the town/ city to answer all the questions. Throw in a few sets of questions relevant to the groom-to-be and test his guests' knowledge of his friend.

## A DAY AT THE RACES

Does the stag have a penchant for betting? This could be the perfect day to suit all the groom-to-be's needs as he enjoys being a part of the exuberant atmosphere, with all his friends in tow. And the good thing is that, depending on your budget, you can spend as much or as little as you feel necessary. The only fixed price is the entry tickets, which vary depending on which races you attend, and any food or drinks you need to buy over the course of the day.

# EVENING ACTIVITIES

## THEATRE

If you want to make a song and dance of this stag do, then why not head to the West End or your home town's theatre district? Whether the groom enjoys a lively musical performance, a dramatic and emotional play or a powerful and moving opera, make sure it's a show-stopper. Although the best seats in the house may cost an arm and a leg, cheaper tickets are always available, especially if you book early. It's a good idea to buy the tickets as far in advance as possible, but make sure the groom-to-be is 100 per cent fixed on this idea before purchasing them.

## FINE DINING

Although the name suggests exclusivity, there are many 'daily deal' companies, such as Wowcher and Voucher Cloud, which offer superb three-course dining deals. Often these deals include the price of a theatre ticket so make sure you do your research before making a reservation or booking at the box office. If you build in some free activities earlier in the day, the cost of this super-sophisticated evening won't put a dent in your wallets.

## STAG HACK

If you want to keep the costs down, how about creating the perfect bachelor evening by hiring a small function room in a members' or golf club. Settle in and enjoy the luxuries of leather chairs and a roaring fire as you host a poker night. Make sure you have chipped in for some fine whiskies and gin, and learn how to make some cocktails fit for gentlemen so you can teach your guests. Don't forget the finger food!

Whether you want to play cards or poker, or you are happy just sharing stories round the table, this hack could be the perfect way for an evening of luxury without too much expense.

## ESSENTIAL KIT

★ Smart clothes (they don't necessarily have to be expensive)

★ Fine food and drink

★ A taste for the high life

## FANCY DRESS

★ Top hats and walking sticks

★ Period costumes

★ Artist (smock and beret essential, moustache optional)

# THEME: PETROLHEAD

---

**IF EVERYTHING IS UNDER CONTROL, YOU ARE NOT MOVING FAST ENOUGH.**

★ *Mario Andretti* ★

---

Whether it involves tiny Minis or massive tanks, make your groom-to-be's stag do an exhilarating experience with a petrol-fuelled activity. There is plenty to choose from, depending on what kind of motor and levels of adrenaline you think the group can stomach. Activities aren't split into daytime and night-time categories in this chapter, as most of the events for this theme occur through the day.

# ACTIVITIES

## STUNT DRIVING

Does the groom-to-be think he's a bit of a James Bond? Have him speed his way round a track doing donuts, handbrake turns and high-speed parallel parking to see if this is true or not. Even if he isn't quite as gifted as he thought he'd be, at least you know he's had a great time regardless. Specifically catered for stag dos, some companies have created a competition where the stag and the best man each lead a team to try to get over the finish line first.

## BUGGY RACING

Think *Mad Max*. Yes, that type of buggy. An off-road course of buggy racing might be just the thing for the groom-to-be. After you learn the ropes, you'll be able to compete with everyone in time trials and races. Create forfeits and prizes for the losers and winners respectively. If you want to be in the groom-to-be's good books, give him first pole position.

## GO-KARTING

For something as adrenaline-pumping but with a smaller price tag, go-karting for a stag do is a no-brainer. Courses are becoming more and more challenging and many are on multiple levels so you can test your nerve behind the wheel to the max. This is a great activity that appeals to every man's inner speed demon. Once you familiarise yourself with the track, you'll be whizzing round thinking you could give Lewis Hamilton a run for his money.

# CAR SHOW

If the groom-to-be is obsessed with all things motorised, but doesn't necessarily want the thrills of driving a fast car, a car show might tickle his fancy. Tickets are sometimes difficult to come by, especially for renowned events such as Goodwood Revival, but if you are organised you should be able to reserve them. Schedule a full day for this, as there is usually so much to do, including watching races, looking at the beautiful cars on display, enjoying the atmosphere and having a few bevvies.

Depending on what type of car show you are attending, this activity is the perfect excuse to dress up. If you think the groom-to-be would prefer going to a vintage car exhibition, check with the guests to see if they'd want to go in authentic period costumes. Ranging from the flying forties to the swinging sixties, there are countless outfits to choose from and if you search hard enough you could find suitable items at a charity shop or a car-boot sale. If the groom-to-be would be more interested in a modern-day car event, dressing up in race or rally suits would perfectly complement the day.

# HIRE A LIMO

Or, if you want something a little different, there are plenty of cars you can choose from to hire. Kick back and relax as you are chauffeured around the city, drinking in the sights and drinking up the alcohol, stopping at any bars you wish to go to.

# ROAD TRIP

If the groom-to-be is planning an intimate affair with a handful of people for his stag do and you know he loves to explore and discover new places, then perhaps a road trip would be the perfect getaway for him. Hire a campervan or a Land Rover and roam your home country or the roads of a foreign country. Campervans usually come with the choice to add extras so if there are slightly more people than places to sleep you could always pay for an awning so you don't feel so cramped. If you want to do a road trip abroad, make sure you check out the county's rules and regulations for driving there. Be sure to plan the route properly and don't try to fit too much into your schedule. Drive through beautiful countryside or along stunning coastal routes through the day, stopping off whenever you feel like it, and sleep under the stars at night. This is the ultimate trip for any keen explorer.

## STAG HACK

Does anyone you know or do any of the guests know someone who has a flash car they'd be willing to drive you around in for the night instead of having to fork out an arm and a leg to hire a car from a company? This is a cheap way of having a night of luxury and sophistication, but decide the route and how long you expect to be out before you ask the favour. Offer the driver some money for their generosity and split the cost with the guests. Don't forget to create a playlist that includes the groom-to-be's favourite and most-hated songs, then wind down the windows and sing along to your hearts' content.

# ESSENTIAL KIT

★ No fear
★ Comfy clothing
★ Driving licences

# FANCY DRESS IDEAS

★ F1 drivers
★ Presenters of *Top Gear* or *The Grand Tour*
★ Period costumes

# THEME: FOODIE

---

**ONE CANNOT THINK WELL, LOVE WELL, SLEEP WELL, IF ONE HAS NOT DINED WELL.**

★ *Virginia Woolf* ★

---

Whether the groom-to-be enjoys the experience of haute cuisine or the pleasure of socialising over an array of traditional restaurant dishes with his closest pals, you'll find something to nourish the soul with this section of delectable activities.

# DAYTIME ACTIVITIES

## FOOD FESTIVAL

With various food and drink festivals taking place throughout the year you'll have no trouble finding something to suit your date and location. What better way to pass an afternoon than wandering around food and drink stalls and sampling the fare on offer. Many food festivals also provide entertainment to add to the party atmosphere.

## COOKERY COURSE

Does the groom-to-be see himself as a bit of a Gordon Ramsay? Or does he wish he could make a Victoria sponge as good as Mary Berry's? Choose a cookery class and learn some new culinary skills to impress your partner with. Depending on what type of cooking the stag prefers – posh nosh or pasties – there'll be a course out there for him. Most companies will offer nibbles and alcohol of your choice while you watch and learn from an experienced chef. It is likely that you will get the chance to taste your masterpieces at the end. *Bon appetit*!

## PIZZA-MAKING

If you and your friends all enjoy devouring pizzas during the big match, a pizza-making class is just the thing for you. In a relaxed environment, you will learn how to make and toss dough to create the perfect base, and then add your favourite fresh toppings. After you've cooked it to a sizzling success, reap your rewards and tuck in with a refreshing pint. If you are feeling generous share your slices with the rest of the group.

## STAG HACK

If your kitchen is a suitable size for a group of well-fed men and you don't mind it getting a little bit messy, you could consider hosting your very own pizza party. Ensure you've practised a few times so you are confident that you could teach the group the basics of pizza-making. Turn the cookery class into a competition whereby the guests have to create a scene, or a portrait of the groom-to-be, with the toppings. Award the winner with a prize and the loser with a nasty alcoholic concoction. Make sure everyone comes in their makeshift chef's whites to have everyone looking and feeling the part, and create a playlist of cheesy Italian pop music to give the evening an authentic ambience.

# HUNT, SKIN AND COOK

Is the groom-to-be a hands-on kind of guy? Does he like to know where his food has come from? With this activity, he'll definitely know where it's from as you hunt and gather wild produce to make your very own meal with. During a full day, you will learn how to make traps for small to large animals, catch fish, skin and cut the carcass of an animal, build a fire, cook the meat and forage wild plants to complete the dish. The activity aims to help you learn the basics of self-sufficiency, as well as having a laugh with friends in a relaxed environment. Before you book, speak to all the guests and check if they are happy to partake. If there are vegetarians or vegans in the group, they may not want to be involved in the day for the obvious reasons. If you want to prolong the feeling of being at one with nature, look for an event that includes camping out under the stars. You will be taught how to make a shelter that is good enough to sleep in – but remember to keep the fire alight otherwise it might get a tad chilly. Then, in the morning, you can start your day by foraging berries for breakfast, making sure they aren't poisonous first, of course!

# EVENING ACTIVITIES

## FOOD CHALLENGE

Ever watched *Man v Food* with the groom-to-be and thought you could polish off a mountain of greasy, stodgy but heavenly junk food? Now is your chance to put it to the test. Make sure you have empty stomachs as you sit down for a memorable feast. Most restaurants/pubs that offer this challenge will offer a couple of alternatives and prizes are usually awarded to winners, or they get the meal for free.

Alternatively, you could create the same event in the comfort of your own home. Cook pizzas or a vat of curry in advance and then let the eating competition commence. Record the efforts on your phone so that you can all laugh about it later on – that's if you aren't stuck on the toilet of course!

If you want to try something a bit different that is just as challenging but won't have you loosening your belt, you could choose a type of food that is incredibly hot or dry and see how much of it you can consume. For example, the challenge could be to see who can eat the most chillies or cream crackers in a certain time limit.

Make sure you haven't booked a strenuous activity to follow this as the do might end in tears and tummy aches.

## MEDIEVAL BANQUET

Step back in time to the courts of yore and be dazzled by fine wine and a spread of traditional dishes. This evening will see you waited on by beautiful women and entertained by rambunctious jesters and jousting knights. Be sure to dress up accordingly for this activity. Let the groom-to-be have reigning position as the mad king, equipped with a crown and staff, and make sure at least one of the group comes as a jester. Give the king his rightful status and let him make up a set of rules that the rest of the stags must abide by throughout the evening to add an extra level of mischief and fun.

## STEAK AND STRIP

If the stag is into his food but he's a bit shy when it comes to a proper sit-down three-course meal, make this a cliché he'll remember by organising a meal with a scantily clad, dancing woman as his side order. This is your chance to embarrass the groom-to-be as much as you can, and don't forget to film it all, that is, of course, if the stripper gives you permission to.

## ESSENTIAL KIT

★ An empty stomach

★ Elasticated waistband

★ Apron and chef's hat for cooking challenges

★ Outdoor gear for hunting activities

## FANCY DRESS IDEAS

★ Medieval

★ Hunters/cavemen

★ Crazy chefs for the stags, sexy waitress for the groom-to-be

# THEME: SPORTY

---

**DO YOU KNOW WHAT MY FAVOURITE PART OF THE GAME IS? THE OPPORTUNITY TO PLAY.**

★ *Mike Singletary* ★

---

Sport unites people all over the world so get the stag do off to a head start with activities that will have your guests cheering all day and all night. The options are endless, from booking football match tickets to playing golf or swapping land for some extreme water sports. Speak to the guests prior to booking to check if they have any medical conditions or preferences that might inhibit them from partaking in an activity.

# DAYTIME ACTIVITIES

## PLAY FOOTBALL WITH A LEGEND

This comes with a big price tag but if you're willing to pay you could go down in history as the best best man there has ever been. You will meet a footballing legend on the pitch where you can play a match, take penalties or just mess about with the ball. Afterwards, you'll be able to sit down with a pint and find out all about his career and life as a footballer.

# SURFING

Whether you are a pro or you've never surfed in your life, this activity is always great for those with bundles of energy. With locations all across the world, you can be specific with your search, from the climate to the size of the waves. Some of the top places to surf are Hanalei in Hawaii, Biarritz in France, Muizenburg in South Africa and Thurso in Scotland. Make sure that your fellow stags are happy with the cost of the activity, flights and accommodation before you commit. If the party is keen on the idea of surfing but can't afford the package you are offering, look locally as there are likely to be more options to choose from than you might think.

It's usually better to go for a weekend course, provided the other stags approve, to really be able to improve. Take a GoPro so you can play back the videos that same evening and have a laugh at your surf fails. If you want to continue the fun into the night, choose a surf destination that is known for its party life. You might be hungover the next day but you'll soon be cured once you take a dip in the sea.

# GOLF

Don your best patterned jumpers and get straight on to the fairway if you know the stag would love nothing more than spending his weekend hitting birdies. This is a great activity for home or abroad and there are plenty of courses to choose from. If you are all experienced golfers, you might want to spend a whole weekend teeing off in the day and settling down with a few beers in the evening. Or, if you haven't had much practice before there are always options for the novices, such as minigolf, the driving range or a golf simulator. For some relaxation and lads' time away, this is an easy choice, especially if the rest of the group are as big on golf as the groom-to-be.

# WATER SPORTS

Whether sun-drenched or rain-drenched, a great activity for sporting fanatics is water sports, whether you fancy some light kayaking and paddleboarding or some extreme jet skiing and wakeboarding. If you've never done anything like it before this could be the perfect time to take the plunge. Book at a water sports centre which offers a range of activities so that the guests have the option to choose what they want to do.

# EVENING ACTIVITIES

## TICKETS TO A SPORTING EVENT

Whether the groom-to-be is into football, rugby, darts or snooker, surprise him with tickets to a match or competition. Check the fixtures for his favourite team or sportsperson well in advance and book a match that works with his available dates. To purchase tickets, especially if you need a large number of them, it might be best to watch a match against a smaller team or attend a smaller sporting event so that seats aren't as limited.

## PUB GOLF

You don't have to be a fan of golf to play just so long as you are a fan of drinking. Pub golf is a game in which players visit a set number of pubs and have to drink the alcoholic beverage that is shown on their scorecard. Make sure you tell everyone about what you have in store so that they have enough time to rustle up a golfing costume. Decide whether you want to play nine or eighteen holes (i.e. go to nine or eighteen pubs) and create a scorecard for each player. To get a par for each hole you have to drink the given beverage in the number of gulps that is next to the drink's name on the scorecard.

# STAG HACK

Example of a pub golf scorecard

| Drinker's Names: | | | | |
|---|---|---|---|---|
| Hole | Pub Name | Type of Drink | Par | Score |
| 1 | | | | |
| 2 | | | | |
| 3 | | | | |
| 4 | | | | |
| 5 | | | | |
| 6 | | | | |
| 7 | | | | |
| 8 | | | | |
| 9 | | | | |
| 10 | | | | |
| 11 | | | | |
| 12 | | | | |
| 13 | | | | |
| 14 | | | | |
| 15 | | | | |
| 16 | | | | |
| 17 | | | | |
| 18 | | | | |
| | | TOTAL | | |

# ESSENTIAL KIT

★ Sportswear

★ Lots of energy

★ Competitiveness

# FANCY DRESS IDEAS

★ Kit of the groom-to-be's favourite team

★ Celebrity sportspeople

★ Pub golf outfit

# THEME: MUSIC

---

## NEXT TO MUSIC, BEER WAS BEST.

★ *Carson McCullers* ★

---

Does the groom-to-be live his life through music? Does he attach a song to each memorable event he's experienced? Organise a music-themed stag do for him and, if you want to make it even more special, base it around the era or genre of music he loves the most.

# DAYTIME ACTIVITIES

## RECORDING STUDIO EXPERIENCE

Is the guest of honour a born performer? If so, why not investigate hiring a recording studio for a day or afternoon. Not only will he feel like a rock 'n' roll star for the day, you could also lay down some tracks for you all to keep as a memento of the weekend. Dress up as your favourite artists to add to the fun and make sure someone films the stag singing and dancing to show his lovely wife-to-be before the big day.

## MUSICAL PILGRIMAGE

Is the groom-to-be a huge fan of a world-famous band or solo artist? Look out for special tours where you'll be able to learn everything there is to know about their idols, find out how they lived and go to their favourite music haunts. There is a popular Beatles tour in Liverpool where you can visit the Cavern Club and step on board the Magical Mystery Tour Bus. If you spend some time searching the internet a host of alternative artists are bound to pop up.

## GO TO A MUSIC FESTIVAL

The peak wedding season usually coincides with several major music festivals, so why not take the stag do to Glastonbury (or something a little easier to get hold of tickets for and perhaps more local to you)? There are festivals of all shapes and sizes, to fit every budget and music taste. You don't have to restrict yourself to local music festivals – you could also include this as part of a trip abroad if your budget will stretch.

## STAG HACK

Is the groom-to-be a music buff, but the party budget won't stretch to a music festival-fuelled weekend? Then why not create your own! Do any of the stags have friends in bands? If they're up for it, get them to play. Or, if you really want a live band to play for you but you don't know any musicians, you could always hire a local band for the evening, which won't cost too much if split between the group. Otherwise, check out your local pubs and bars and see if they have live music scheduled for the weekend of the stag do. Whether you are creating your own DIY music festival indoors or outside, don't forget to wear your wellies and plastic poncho for the occasion!

# EVENING ACTIVITIES

## KARAOKE NIGHT

Warm up those lungs and put on some funky sunglasses and feather boas (earplugs are optional) as you sing the night away. If you know your local pub is holding a karaoke event, this could be great for saving some pennies as they are usually free, or you could hire a private karaoke room, such as Lucky Voice, if you want a more intimate affair. Make sure you agree on a classic song you all love so that you can belt it out together for the finale performance. Whoever hasn't learnt the words gets a forfeit!

## MUSIC CONCERT

If you have a big budget, book tickets to see a household name; maybe you could even stretch to going to see them abroad if they are doing a world tour and the only date available to you is when they're in a different country. Or, if you are looking for something a little more low-key, there are so many options available in smaller venues all over the UK. You never know, you might even see a band in a tiny club that end up being as big as The Beatles in years to come!

# ESSENTIAL KIT

★ Angelic voices

★ A rock 'n' roll attitude

★ Epic dance moves

# FANCY DRESS IDEAS

★ Favourite artists

★ Artists from a certain era/genre

★ Big, colourful wigs, inflatable guitars and wacky sunglasses

# THEME:
# BUDGET

---

**FRUGALITY INCLUDES ALL
THE OTHER VIRTUES.**

★ *Cicero* ★

---

What with all the costs of the wedding, sometimes the groom-to-be has to be realistic with what he can spend on his stag do. If the guests are strapped for cash, this is another reason to organise something a little more low-key. Even though you won't be partaking in extravagant activities, the groom-to-be will still have an awesome time just by being able to spend it with all his friends and loved ones. Here are some budget ideas to keep the group entertained.

# DAYTIME ACTIVITIES

## ESCAPE ROOM

These are pretty new to the stag do scene but they are becoming increasingly popular. Together, you must work as a team to solve clues that will allow you to escape the room. You only have a certain timeframe in which to complete all the puzzles, and if you run out of time you'll be locked in forever (or until a member of staff retrieves you). If you are a big group, split into teams and see which one manages to do it in the quickest time. It's fun, and better still it's cheap!

# PAINTBALLING

This is a real crowd-pleaser and always great value for money no matter which venue you go to. Paintballing favours those with lots of banter, a streak of competitiveness, a high pain threshold and bundles of energy. Split into teams and make it your mission to win. Afterwards, you can compare bruises over a beer.

Alternatively, laser quest also offers plenty of fun for a small cost, but without being pummelled by paintballs. If you don't want the groom-to-be's partner thinking that the stag do involved you taking advantage of him then this might be a better option for all.

# TEN-PIN BOWLING

Everyone loves ten-pin bowling, especially when everyone is a group of guys that is up for some laughs and a few pints. Introduce prizes for the winners and those who get strikes, and forfeits for the losers and those who get gutter balls. End the day with a few goes on the arcade games – the air-hockey machine is a must!

As an alternative, how about playing ten-pin bowling with a twist. Instead of throwing balls at the pins, why don't you have a go at being the pins and balls yourselves with human ten-pin bowling. Don't fret, as all the equipment is inflatable so when you fall down it isn't going to hurt. Of course, this activity will be more expensive than the total cost of a couple of games of bowling but it does guarantee laughs aplenty.

# EVENING ACTIVITIES

## MAGIC EVENING

Make magic à la Dynamo and host an evening of surprises and tricks. Buy a couple of home magic kits and practise perfecting the art of magic together. End the evening with a bang and have your own firework display. Don't forget the sparklers so you can write each other's names in the air (or draw inappropriate body parts). Even though the groom-to-be is taking the next big step in his life, he's probably still a child at heart.

# MURDER MYSTERY

You can buy or download a good murder mystery game from the internet for around £20. There are lots of different stories and each game caters for different numbers of people so double check you have bought one that is relevant to your stag do. A murder mystery is a party game where one of the players is secretly, and unknowingly, playing a murderer. The other attendees must determine who among them is the criminal and at the end of the game they all say who they think is the murderer (at this point the actual murderer will know it is them and will have to dissuade the others from believing it is them). Make the game more realistic (or funny, as you please) by dressing up as your characters and sustaining the relevant accents during the whole game.

## STAG HACK

Before you book anything through a company, check if there's another company which offers a similar product for a small amount of the price. Don't settle for the first activity you stumble upon, but contact a number of places to get a rough idea of how much each will cost and make sure that the quotes include all the added extras so that you don't get stung by any additional extras on the day. A good place to start your search is on websites such as Voucher Cloud and Voucher Codes, which have offers and discounts running throughout the year. Do your research and you might end up getting more for your money than you thought you would.

# ESSENTIAL KIT

★ An empty wallet (maybe take a few notes with you)

★ Good negotiating skills

★ A creative mind for coming up with alternatives to expensive activities (the internet is great for helping you out if you are stuck for ideas)

# FANCY DRESS IDEAS

★ Anything and everything that's cheap (head to your local charity shops for inspiration)

★ Murder mystery characters

★ Military wear

★ Classic American bowling gear

★ A magician's outfit

# LOCATIONS

# UK

THE LANDSCAPE AT ITS
FINEST POSSESSES A QUALITY
THAT THE LANDSCAPES
OF OTHER NATIONS...
INEVITABLY FAIL TO POSSESS.

★ *Kazuo Ishiguro* ★

## TOP STAG DO DESTINATIONS IN THE UK

★ Aberdeen

★ Bath

★ Belfast

★ Birmingham

★ Brighton

★ Bristol

★ Blackpool

★ Cambridge

★ Cardiff

★ Chelsea

★ Chester

★ Edinburgh

★ Essex

★ Glasgow

★ London

★ Manchester

★ Newcastle

★ Newquay

★ Oxford

★ York

# WHERE TO GO?

Take a look at the most popular destinations on the opposite page and peruse the pages relating to the suggested themes. Marry the two together and you should be closer to finding a good fit. Whether the groom-to-be would prefer a city break, all-night clubbing, culture, or nature and tranquillity are all things to consider. Think about costs, too. If you are on a budget, check which locations are the cheapest for accommodation and what type of accommodation would be suitable for a self-catered experience. Ask the stags for some inspiration if you're feeling stumped and see where the suggestions lead you.

# WHERE TO STAY?

Once you've decided on a location, think about the accommodation that would best suit your party. In a city centre, you might want to rent a house or apartment and in the countryside you may prefer a cottage. Alternatively, you might want to stay in a hotel or B&B, or perhaps you'd rather stay at a campsite or in a forest or, if you're on a budget, there are youth hostels. Maybe you'd all rather take to the water and stay on a boat. Whatever you decide, there are plenty of websites out there that will make your job of finding the perfect place that much easier. Check the resources section at the back of the book for more information.

# WHEN TO GO?

Make sure the chosen location and the activities fit the weather. If the groom-to-be wants to go camping in Scotland, for example, a December weekend is out of the question. If you're planning a winter stag do, make sure people will still be able to get there whatever the weather – even if it snows.

Think about if you want to cut costs by avoiding school holidays. If the majority of you don't have children or have someone who can look after them while you are away, this could save everyone a great deal of money.

If you are travelling a long way to get to your destination, think about the day and time you will be travelling. Late afternoons and early evenings on Fridays are probably not the most ideal time as people are more likely to be on the roads. Another time to avoid travelling, if you are going by car or coach, is during major national holidays, such as Easter or Christmas.

# ORGANISING THE STAGS

★ Ensure all stags are aware of any extra items/props they need to bring or purchase themselves.

★ Work out how much everything is going to cost and let the stags know in advance how much money they will need to bring.

★ Make sure everyone is aware of any themes/fancy dress ideas.

★ Are you going anywhere that requires a dress code? Make sure all stags know what's expected of them on this front.

★ Send out detailed instructions on how to get to the venue.

# STAG HACK

If you are travelling from the same area, organise a car share or purchase train tickets altogether, as you can usually receive a discount if you buy as a group. There are also super-save options to choose from, where you select a specific time to travel for a cheaper fee. Always check train timetables before booking to make sure there are no rail improvement works scheduled for the date(s) when you are travelling.

Alternatively, you could make your journey via coach. There are plenty of coach companies that offer a number of deals across the country so check these out before you buy. It might also be worth looking into hiring a minivan. If you're travelling around a lot during the stag do this might cut costs further instead of paying for public transport services. Before you hire the van, check that there is one willing person who you can appoint as designated driver. If you know the stag do is going to be boozy, it's not worth the risk of driving the day after a heavy night.

# ABROAD

---

**THE WORLD IS A BOOK, AND THOSE WHO DO NOT TRAVEL READ ONLY ONE PAGE.**

★ *Proverb* ★

---

## TOP STAG DO DESTINATIONS OVERSEAS

★ Algarve

★ Amsterdam

★ Barcelona

★ Bratislava

★ Budapest

★ Dublin

★ Hamburg

★ Ibiza

★ Krakow

★ Las Vegas

★ Magaluf

★ Prague

★ Riga

★ Tallinn

★ Valencia

# WHERE TO GO?

Take a look at the most popular stag do destinations abroad (see previous page) for some inspiration and take a look through the chapters describing different themes. Marry the two together and you should be well on your way to the perfect stag do. Does the groom-to-be want guaranteed sunshine? Does he want culture or the beach? Nightclubs and foam parties or natural beauty and tranquillity? Ask the other stags for some inspiration if you get stuck and together you'll come to the right decision.

# WHERE TO STAY?

There are plenty of online resources to help you with this one, whether you opt for a villa, hotel, an apartment or a youth hostel. Always book as far in advance as possible as the closer you leave it to your arrival date the more expensive the prices will be, not to mention that good deals sell out very quickly. Look at some of the many hotel deals websites for help and advice on all your accommodation needs. This includes researching customer reviews as you'll be able to gauge if the accommodation is suitable for a stag do. If you aren't sure, always ring the company before you book, as some hotels or apartments might have a strictly no-stag-and-hen-do rule.

# WHEN TO GO?

When organising a stag do abroad, it's important to remember to keep costs down. As the plan starts to take shape, you don't want guests to start dropping out because the financial impact is spiralling out of control. For this reason, it makes sense to avoid school holidays (and bank holidays, where possible), book flights and accommodation as far in advance as you can (and look out for discount codes and cashback offers – savings you can pass on to the stags) and arrange to pay for the accommodation after booking to spread the cost over a few months.

# THINGS TO CONSIDER

★ Are you travelling via a budget airline? If hold luggage costs extra, make sure each guest has told you whether they want to bring anything other than cabin baggage. Warn everyone that if they don't opt in now and then turn up with a big suitcase on the day, they will have to cough up for it.

★ Remind all the guests to check their passport is in date – it's recommended that travellers have at least six months left on their passport before going abroad.

★ Make sure all the stags are aware of any props, items or outfits they need to bring with them and make sure everyone has room in their luggage. If you are only taking cabin baggage, make sure you know what you can and can't take on the plane with you.

★ Before you all head out, it's a sensible idea to organise a meeting place in case people get lost or at least make sure everyone has the phone numbers of whoever are the keyholders of the accommodation.

★ Remind people to be sensible when it comes to their personal belongings – tourists are often targeted by pickpockets so everyone should carry around a photocopy of their passport (leaving the real thing back at the accommodation, unless you need it for ID and nothing else will do), and have their wits about them.

★ Men can get their drink spiked as well as women, so remind the stags not to leave their drinks unattended. Stick together!

★ Plan ahead and book restaurants, clubs and bars. Do some research and make sure there are plenty of places that accept large single-sex groups.

# WHAT TO DO IF YOU LOSE YOUR PASSPORT

★ Before leaving the country, email a photo/scan of your passport to yourself. Take a photo of it with your phone so it's on there too.

★ Carry a printout of your travel itinerary, along with a passport photo and driver's licence – in case you need to acquire an emergency replacement passport.

★ Make sure you have the telephone number of your home country's embassy – in the event that you lose your passport, they will be able to help you.

★ If you believe you have lost your passport, don't panic and check absolutely everywhere before raising the alarm. File a police report if you believe your passport has been stolen.

# THINGS TO MAKE AND DO

# GAMES

---

**LIFE IS MORE FUN IF YOU PLAY GAMES.**

★ *Roald Dahl* ★

---

# THINGS TO TAKE INTO CONSIDERATION

★ How well do the guests know each other? Will anyone mind sharing sensitive information with people they've just met?

★ Are there any family members present? Would the groom-to-be prefer things were kept 'clean'?

★ Are there many non-drinkers? If so, don't gear all the games around alcohol.

★ Make sure games are appropriate for the stags' ages and personality types.

★ Is the venue suitable for the games in question?

★ How long will the games take and will they work with other activities planned?

# DRINKING GAMES

**Banned words** – Choose a word or phrase that is off limits for the night or the entire weekend, whatever you think will work best. This could be anything from the stag's name to 'drink' or 'wedding'. Players will need to come up with alternative words for whatever has been banned and whoever drops the banned word over the course of the game needs to then take a drink or do a shot.

**Flip or strip** – All you need is a coin and some nerves of steel to play this game. Flip a coin and the person to your left shouts heads or tails. If they answer correctly, they have to sip their drink; if they are incorrect, the penalty is to remove an item of clothing.

**Never have I ever...** – In this game players sit in a circle and take it in turns to admit to something they have never done. This can be hugely embarrassing or just something like 'I have never been on a stag do' or 'I have never been on a motorbike', and whoever has done that thing must take a drink or do a shot. In games like this where a lot of drinking is likely to be involved, you're better off setting the drink people need to take as either a sip or two fingers.

**Shark attack** – The nominated shark spotter will shout 'Shark attack!' and the rest of the group have to lie on the floor as quickly as they can. You could be anywhere – at the groom-to-be's house, in the pub, in the street or mid-activity. The last to lie down must down a drink and then they become the shark spotter.

**Name that drink** – Here's one to get the groom-to-be's taste buds working hard. Organise for each guest to bring an alcoholic drink. Blindfolded, the stag must take a shot of each drink. If they get it wrong another shot of said drink is poured into a pint glass. Once the game has finished, the groom-to-be must down the dirty pint in one.

**Vodka roulette** – Take ten identical shot glasses and fill half of them with water and half with vodka. Each person must take it in turns to choose a glass and drink the contents. Someone needs to be in charge for this one and to avoid the others seeing you pour out the drinks, perhaps you could get them to all face the other way or, even better, to play the game blindfolded and choose the glasses by number. You can choose the number of rounds you play in advance or until someone gives up.

**'Roxanne'** – One of the best drinking games ever concocted. For this one all you'll need is a full glass, a chair/sitting place each and 'Roxanne' by The Police at the ready, either via a stereo or, if desperate, via your mobile phone. Split the players into two teams – one team is assigned the lyric 'Roxanne' and the other team takes 'red light'. Whenever Sting sings 'Roxanne', the team of the same name must stand up and take a drink and sit down again and whenever he sings 'red light' the other team must get up from their seat and take a swig. Best played only once of an evening.

**Fuzzy duck** – Start the game with everyone sitting in a circle and taking it in turns to say 'fuzzy duck'. If someone says 'Does he?', you must switch the direction and say 'Ducky fuzz' until the next person says 'Does he?' and the game is reversed. Every time someone makes a mistake – and don't worry, you'll know when that happens – they drink and the game starts again.

# NON-DRINKING GAMES

**Name in a hat** – Split the party into two teams and hand each player three scraps of paper and a pen. Ask each stag to write down the names of three different people – real or fictional, alive or dead – fold it up and put it in a large bowl. No one must reveal their name to anyone else. This game consists of three rounds, in which players from each team take it in turns to take names from the hat, offer clues to their teammates and allow them to guess the name in question. Each player has a 30-second slot and teams should alternate as it is important that everyone is listening the whole time. Here's the twist. The round is over when all names have been removed from the hat – then they must be refolded and placed back in the bowl. In round one you can use as many words as you like to describe the person as long as you do not actually say their name; in round two you may use only three words to describe the person; and in round three you may only describe that person using noises or gestures. Players are allowed to pass, but each correct guess equals a point, which will be added up at the end to determine who has won.

**Sticky-note game** – Write the name of a famous person – real or fictional, alive or dead – on a sticky note and stick to the forehead of the person opposite you. Once everyone has a name stuck to their forehead the game can begin. Players take it in turns to ask questions about the person whose name is attached to their forehead. They can ask as many questions as they like until they get a 'no' answer and then the questioning moves round to the next player. The last person to guess correctly loses the game.

**Name that food/drink** – Place various foods and drinks in bowls and cups on a table. Someone will need to be in charge. Blindfold the players and get them to taste the various foodstuffs and beverages, guessing what they are. Whoever guesses the most correctly wins the game.

**How many pegs…?** – Sort of like human Buckaroo, see how many pegs you can attach to other stags without them realising. Whoever secures the most pegs wins the game. This is a good one to play alongside another game, so everyone is distracted and so hopefully not realising when they're being pegged! Buy pegs in a selection of sizes and assign a points system, so giant pegs score the highest and miniature pegs score fewer points. Hand out the pegs and make sure everyone writes their initials on each peg in their collection so points can be tallied up at the end.

**Spank it** – You will need a deck of cards and a table-tennis bat for this game. The dealer shuffles the cards and lays seven of them face down in a row on a flat surface. The player must take a card from the deck and guess whether the first card in the row will be higher or lower than it. If they guess correctly, then they must decide whether the second card in the row is higher or lower than the previous card that has been turned over. If and when they guess incorrectly, the dealer gets to spank the player on their backside with the table-tennis bat.

**Toy soldiers** – Buy a pack of toy soldiers and put them in a plastic bag. Ask each stag to pick a toy soldier from the bag – whichever position the soldier is holding this will be that stag's soldier position for the rest of the stag do. Continue the antics of the day as per normal, but whenever the groom-to-be calls 'Assume the position' each stag must drop whatever they are doing and hold their toy soldier pose. Whoever fails to do so must pay the price with a truth or dare.

**Down, Mr President** – This is another funny game that you can keep playing at random points of the stag do. When someone shouts 'Down, Mr President!' all the stags must pounce on the groom-to-be to protect him. The last to protect the groom-to-be must complete a forfeit.

# GAMES ABOUT THE GROOM-TO-BE

**Mr & Mrs** – This one takes a bit of organisation but is well worth it. Come up with a list of questions about the groom-to-be's partner and ask them to provide the answers. Even better – film it on your phone (or ask the partner to) and get someone to bring a laptop/tablet or pipe it into the TV, so you can play their responses to him at the stag do. Ask the groom-to-be each question, wait for his response and then play his partner's response. If he answers incorrectly he should take a drink or do a shot.

**How well do you know the groom-to-be?** – Turning the previous game around, you could organise for the groom-to-be to answer a list of questions about himself (and film him answering them) and then ask the stags to take it in turns answering the questions. Whoever answers incorrectly must have a drink or do a shot.

# COCKTAIL RECIPES

---

**CANDY IS DANDY BUT
LIQUOR IS QUICKER.**

★ *Ogden Nash* ★

---

It wouldn't be a stag do without a drink. But why stick to beer when you have the world of mixology at your fingertips? If you think you can host a party good enough for Gatsby himself, use this chapter to cater for everyone, from the hard drinkers to the teetotallers. All recipes are for one serving unless otherwise indicated, so feel free to multiply the quantities in order to create pitchers full of cocktail fun for your group of stags!

# ALCOHOLIC COCKTAILS

## OLD-FASHIONED

### REQUIRED:

1 sugar cube or ½ teaspoon of caster sugar, 3 dashes of aromatic bitters, dash of carbonated water (optional), ice, 60 ml whiskey (rye or bourbon)

# METHOD:

1. Put the sugar into a glass.

2. Add the aromatic bitters; if new to this repertoire of flavours stick to Angostura bitters, but if you'd like to be adventurous there are lots of others on the market for you to experiment with.

3. Top up with carbonated water (optional).

4. Muddle the sugar while rotating the glass at an angle so that the sugar grains and bitters create a lining.

5. Add ice.

6. Finally, pour in the whiskey of your choice, whether it be rye or bourbon.

7. Serve with the old-time charm of a Kentucky gentleman.

# FRENCH 75

## REQUIRED:

35 ml gin, 8 ml sugar syrup (one part water and one part sugar), 15 ml fresh lemon juice, champagne or any white sparkling wine, a twist of lemon rind

## METHOD:

1. Mix the gin, syrup and lemon juice into the shaker, add ice and shake.

2. Strain into a glass.

3. Top up the rest of the glass with champagne, or sparkling wine, which is just as good but a much cheaper alternative.

4. Garnish with the lemon twist, rubbing the excess juice around the rim.

5. Protect yourself in the event of it blowing your roof off.

# TOM COLLINS

## REQUIRED:

60 ml dry gin, 30 ml fresh lemon juice, 1 tsp caster sugar, dash of carbonated water, maraschino cherry, orange twist

## METHOD:

1. Add the gin, lemon juice and sugar in a shaker filled with ice and shake well.

2. Strain into the glass.

3. Top up with carbonated water and stir.

4. Garnish with the cherry and the orange slice, squeezing it first to infuse a zesty flavour.

5. Raise your glass to Tom for the cocktail recipe and the groom-to-be for making the stag do possible.

# LAST WORD

## REQUIRED:

35 ml gin, 35 ml maraschino liqueur,
35 ml green Chartreuse, ice, 1 lime

## METHOD:

1. Add the first three ingredients into a shaker filled with ice.

2. Cut the lime in half and squeeze the juice into the shaker.

3. Shake well and strain into a glass.

4. Serve to your guests, hoping its strength doesn't act as a conversation-stopper.

# NON-ALCOHOLIC COCKTAILS

Who says the drinkers get all the nice cocktails? Push the boat out and make a bit of an effort for the non-drinkers. There may be a few – whether they are only visiting for the day and needing to drive home, or are simply not bothered about the booze. No one wants to be the odd one out so make sure everyone has a glass of something fruity and delicious in their hand.

# GINGER LIME FIZZ

## REQUIRED:

340 ml ginger beer, 115 ml soda water,
generous squeeze of fresh lime juice,
lime slice for garnish

## METHOD:

1. Combine ingredients in a pitcher and stir well.

2. Serve cold and feel the kick of the fizz without the fuzz of the alcohol.

# SAFE SEX ON THE BEACH

## REQUIRED:

85 ml cranberry juice, 85 ml grapefruit juice, 55 ml peach nectar, 1 maraschino cherry

## METHOD:

1. Pour the juice over ice in a chilled long glass and stir.

2. Garnish with a cherry and serve the innocuous drink to a responsible adult.

# SHIRLEY TEMPLE

## REQUIRED:

60 ml orange juice, 175 ml lemonade,
2 tbsp grenadine, 1 maraschino cherry

## METHOD:

1. Take a tall glass and pour in the orange juice and the lemonade.

2. Add the grenadine and allow the syrup to seep slowly.

3. Visually, it should create layers of the juices.

4. Garnish with the cherry.

# HANGOVER RECIPES

GREASE IS THE ONLY CURE
FOR A HANGOVER.

★ *Cameron Diaz* ★

The morning after the heavy night before, usually the first thing on everyone's mind is food. That or the toilet. If you fancy cooking up some greasy grub instead of facing the fast-food restaurants, give some of the following recipes a go.

# PLAIN AND SIMPLE PORRIDGE

If your tummy's feeling a little delicate, try this safe but still super tasty option.

## INGREDIENTS (serves one)

50 g porridge oats
350 ml milk

## TO SERVE:

2 tbsp Greek yogurt, thinned with a little milk
Honey

1. Combine the oats and milk in a large microwave-proof bowl, then microwave on high for 5 minutes, stirring halfway through. Leave to stand for 2 minutes.

2. Pour into a bowl, spoon yogurt on top and drizzle with honey.

# EASY FRENCH TOAST

This is as simple as A, B, C in cooking terms. A great way to gain some best man points.

## INGREDIENTS (serves 12)

4 eggs
175 ml milk
3 tbsp soft light brown sugar
1 tsp ground nutmeg
12 slices thick white bread

## TO SERVE:

1 tbsp ground cinnamon
Icing sugar
Crispy bacon, blueberries and maple syrup, optional

1. Beat the eggs in a bowl, then add the milk, brown sugar and nutmeg and stir well. Soak each slice of bread in the mixture until saturated.

2. Lightly oil a large frying pan and brown the slices on each side. Serve hot, dusted with icing sugar and cinnamon, with crispy bacon or blueberries and maple syrup if desired.

# ULTIMATE BEANS ON TOAST

A classic recipe with a twist and can be made on all levels of a hangover because it's so simple.

## INGREDIENTS (serves two)

2 eggs
4 slices of bread, fresh is best
1 tbsp olive oil
1 onion, diced
½ tsp ground cumin
½ tsp ground coriander
85 g semi-dried tomatoes from a jar, chopped if large
400 g can baked beans
Butter, for spreading (optional)

## TO SERVE:

Fresh chopped coriander or parsley
Cumin

## METHOD:

1. Bring water to the boil in a saucepan for the eggs and toast the bread. Heat the oil in a frying pan, then add the onion and gently cook for a few minutes until it starts to brown. Mix the spices into the pan and stir briefly. Add the tomatoes and beans and cook until warmed through.

2. Turn down the heat under the saucepan so the water is just simmering, then crack in the eggs and gently poach them until the whites are firm but the yolks are still runny. Layer the beans on to the toast (buttered or unbuttered, as you wish) place the eggs on top.

3. Serve with a sprinkle of extra cumin and coriander or parsley.

# PROTEIN-PACKED PASTA

If you've missed breakfast you can always lean on this dish to start your day and give you a well-needed energy boost.

## INGREDIENTS (serves two)

3 tbsp olive oil
2 chicken breasts, diced
3 rashers bacon, chopped
1 garlic clove, crushed
Salt and freshly ground black pepper
150 ml double cream
250 g farfalle

## TO SERVE:

100 g Cheddar or Parmesan cheese, grated
Handful fresh basil, torn

## **METHOD:**

1. Heat the oil in a frying pan, add the chicken and bacon and cook on a medium-high heat until the chicken is golden-brown and cooked through.

2. Add the garlic and cook for 1 minute. Season with salt and freshly ground black pepper, then add the cream and keep on a low heat.

3. While frying the chicken and bacon, cook the pasta according to packet instructions in a pan of salted boiling water, then drain.

4. Add the creamy chicken and bacon mixture to the cooked, drained pasta and stir well.

5. Serve and garnish with cheese and basil.

# RESOURCES

ORGANISING IS WHAT
YOU DO BEFORE YOU DO
SOMETHING, SO THAT WHEN
YOU DO IT, IT IS NOT ALL
MIXED UP.

★ *A. A. Milne* ★

# ACTIVITIES

**Bar crawl:** www.barcrawlbabes.com

**Beer goggle football:** www.bubble-football.co.uk

**Booze cruise:** www.stagweb.co.uk/stag-nights/
boozecruise.asp

**Brewery experience:** www.brewhouseandkitchen.
com, www.sadlersales.co.uk

**Buggy racing:** www.mudmania.co.uk,
www.intotheblue.co.uk/driving-experiences/
buggies/racing-buggies

**Bushcraft:** www.wholeland.org.uk/stagdo,
www.wildwoodbushcraft.com,
www.adventurebritain.com/activity/bushcraft-and-
survival, www.huntergathercook.com

**Canyoning:** www.canyoningscotland.com,
www.adventureswales.co.uk/canyoning-in-wales

**Car show:** www.carcal.co.uk,
www.classicshowsuk.co.uk/index.asp

**Clay pigeon shooting:** www.thebigshoot.co.uk

# STAG DO PLANNING GUIDE

**Coasteering:** www.xtremecoasteering.co.uk,
www.coasteering-wales.co.uk

**Comedy night:** www.99clubcomedy.com,
www.ticketmaster.co.uk

**Cookery course:** www.undergroundcookeryschool.
com, www.brightoncookeryschool.com/courses/
hens-stags

**Escape room:** www.exitgames.co.uk

**Ghost tour/zombie experience:**
www.hauntedhappenings.co.uk,
www.zombieexperiences.co.uk

**Go-karting:** www.uk-go-karting.com

**Horseracing:** www.britishhorseracing.com/race-info/
fixtures/major-events

**Life drawing:** www.henandstaglifedrawing.co.uk

**Limo/car hire:** www.limohire-sportcarhire.co.uk,
www.limosupermarket.co.uk

**Medieval banquet:** www.freedomltd.com/
stag-activities/medieval-banquet

**Murder Mystery:** www.murdermysterygames.co.uk

**Music Festivals:** www.thefestivalcalendar.co.uk,
www.festicket.com/festivals

# RESOURCES

**Paintballing:** www.ukpaintball.co.uk

**Party bus:** www.partybus.co.uk

**Play football with a legend:**
www.playwithalegend.com

**Recording studio experience:** www.studiostars.co.uk

**Scavenger hunt:** www.xmarksthespot.co.uk,
www.adventureconnections.co.uk

**Stargazing:** www.darkskydiscovery.org.uk,
www.nationaltrust.org.uk/features/top-spots-for-
stargazing

**Steak and strip:** www.chillisauce.co.uk/stag/
strip-dinner

**Stunt driving:** www.stuntdriveuk.com

**Surfing:** www.englishsurfing.org

**Theatre:** www.ticketmaster.co.uk/section/arts-theatre

**White water rafting:** www.chillisauce.co.uk/stag/
white-water-rafting

**Zorbing:** www.zorbing.co.uk

# ACCOMMODATION

**Boats:** www.waterwaysholidays.com,
www.drifters.co.uk

**Campsites:** www.coolcamping.co.uk

**Group accommodation:** www.homeaway.co.uk,
www.groupaccommodation.com, www.airbnb.com,
www.bigholidayhouse.com, www.partyhouses.co.uk

**Hotels/B&Bs:** www.hotels.com, www.trivago.co.uk

**Youth hostels:** www.yha.org.uk, www.hostelworld.com

# TRAVEL

**Flights:** www.skyscanner.net, www.momondo.com

**Taxis:** uber.com

**Trains:** www.nationalrail.co.uk, www.thetrainline.com,
www.eurostar.com/uk-en

**Buses:** www.nationalexpress.com/home.aspx,
uk.megabus.com

**Ferries:** www.ferries.co.uk, www.dfdsseaways.co.uk,
www.brittany-ferries.co.uk

# THE
# BACKPACKER'S
# SURVIVAL
# GUIDE

 EVERYTHING

*you need*

 *to* KNOW

*Tamsin King*

# THE BACKPACKER'S SURVIVAL GUIDE
## Everything You Need to Know

Tamsin King

Paperback
£6.99
ISBN: 978-1-84953-984-5

*Tips and ideas for travelling the world*

So you're off to explore the big, wide world: head filled with possibilities and hiking boots laced.

But a big trip brings big questions, like *how do I go about choosing and packing a bag, how should I handle money abroad*, and *what the hell do I do when my hostel dorm is filled with snorers?* Luckily this handy guide is filled with essential tips, advice and hacks to make your adventures on the road truly unforgettable.

If you're interested in finding out more
about our books, find us on Facebook at
**Summersdale Publishers** and follow us
on Twitter at **@Summersdale**.

# www.summersdale.com